JESUS CHRIST THE HEALER

JIM HARWELL

JESUS CHRIST THE HEALER

JIM HARWELL

Bridge Books
Atlanta · Chicago · Nashville

Bridge Books
4487 Post Place
Nashville, Tenn. 37205

Jesus Christ the Healer. Copyright © 2017 by Jim Harwell

All rights reserved, including the right to reproduce this book or portions thereof in any form whatsoever. For information, address:
Bridge Books Subsidiary Rights Department
4487 Post Place
Nashville, Tenn. 37205

For information about Bridge Books products, books, packages, and special discounts for bulk purchases, please contact Bridge Books info@bridgebooks.org.

Scripture references are taken from the New King James Version. © Thomas Nelson, Inc. 1992.

Cover designed by Alexandre Rito

Manufactured in the United States of America

10 9 8 7 6 5 4 3 2 1

Library of Congress

ISBN-13: 978-0-9855943-8-1

To those who need healing

Contents

	Introduction	11
1	God is the Author & Giver of Life	15
2	God's Will is Health & Healing	21
3	Triple Cure for Man	30
4	Jesus & the Passover: Healing	34
5	How to Receive Healing & Health	39
6	Jesus: God's Will in Action	43
7	The Full Gospel: Forgiveness and Healing	51
8	Healing in the Old Covenant	56
9	Objections to Healing	62
10	Truths & Revelations about Healing	76
11	The Names of God Reveal Healing	81
12	Notes	88
13	Healing Scriptures in Every Book of the Bible	94
	Subject Index	113
	Bibliography	114

Introduction

The great and awesome God Almighty is so glorious, so wonderful, and so powerful, we cannot comprehend it.

He created the universe and wants every person on earth to spend eternity with Him in heaven, a place so glorious, words cannot express it.

We see His glory, wonder, and power in many ways and in many revelations in the Bible. A glorious revelation of Him is found in Exodus 34.

In God's awesome declaration and proclamation of Himself in Exodus 34, we see that He is, gloriously:

merciful and compassionate;
gracious and giving;
longsuffering and slow to anger;
abounding in goodness and lovingkindness;
abounding in truth and faithfulness;
And that He:
keeps mercy for thousands;
forgives iniquity;
forgives transgression;
and forgives sin.

Amen! Glory to God forever!

He is truly an awesome and incredible God, the Lord God Almighty! The Father, Son and Holy Spirit! Glory!

A primary example of His mercy, graciousness, goodness, and more is of course the truth of salvation. He wants to save every person from sin and death and give them eternal, everlasting, divine life.

In a sense, salvation could be described as "healing" of the spirit and soul. In reality, it is much more than that: He gives us a completely new life! We are born again. All things are new. Glory to God!

In simplified terms, He gives us a new spirit, with redemption of our soul (the mind, will, and emotions) and so, so much more.

Salvation is so vast and deep, those who make it to heaven will spend eternity receiving, learning about, and exploring (and more!) God's glorious salvation, divine life, and life everlasting.

Another primary example of His mercy, grace, goodness and more is healing of the body.

Just as he offers "healing" of our spirit and soul, God offers healing of our physical body.

Indeed, God offers complete healing and wholeness in spirit, soul, and body, which we call the full gospel.

When God came to earth as a man, Jesus Christ, we see clearly that He healed those in need. He offered healing of the body as part of God's full gospel, the glorious news of Jesus

Christ, the Lord and Savior. And Jesus Christ is the same yesterday, today, and forever.

We will see in this presentation that God has always offered healing to His people, to those who walk with, know, and obey Him.

Today, in this age of grace, when God's love, mercy, and grace are in abundant supply, His healing is even more available that it was in previous ages.

Let's look at how He declared and proclaimed Himself as recorded in Exodus 34:

> Now the Lord descended in the cloud and stood with him there, and proclaimed the name of the Lord. 6 And the Lord passed before him and proclaimed, 'The Lord, the Lord God, merciful and gracious, longsuffering, abounding in goodness and truth, keeping mercy for thousands, forgiving iniquity and transgression and sin . . .' (Exodus 34:6,7).

A quick outline of God's glorious proclamation; with additional translations of words included:

1. Merciful – also translated "compassionate"
2. Gracious – this Hebrew adjective depicts "a heartfelt response by someone who has something to give to one who has a need," specifically one more powerful than another who has no right to receive the gift.
3. Longsuffering – also translated "slow to an-

ger"

4. Abounding in goodness – also "abundant in lovingkindness"

5. Abounding in truth – also "abundant in faithfulness"

6. Keeping mercy for thousands

7. Forgiving iniquity (see pages 32-33)

8. Forgiving transgression

9. Forgiving sin

God Almighty is merciful, gracious, slow to anger, abounding in goodness, and abounding in truth – and infinitely more.

His glorious promises, truth, revelation and more, such as His glorious promise and revelation of healing, flow from Him and His nature and character.

ONE

God is the Author and Giver of Life

God is the author and giver of life, health, and healing. He is not in any way involved in anything that causes pain, suffering, sickness, or death.

Everything that is good comes from God. Some examples include:
Light – 1 John 1:5
Life – John 1:4
Love – 1 John 4:16
Mercy – Psalm 36:5
Strength – Psalm 18:32
Peace – Isaiah 9:6
Water – Deuteronomy 11:11

Entities such as evil, sickness, and the like originated with the devil and are the result of the fall and sin, which originated with the devil.

All good gifts and all perfect gifts come from God (James 1:17).

James 1:17 – "Every good gift and every perfect gift is from above, and comes down from the Father of lights, with whom there is no variation or shadow of turning."

God is a giving God.

John 3:16 – "For God so loved the world He GAVE His only begotten Son, that whosoever relies on Him shall not perish but have everlasting life."

The hairs upon our heads are numbered. He cares about every detail of our body.

Jesus Christ is God. He healed and went about doing good.

Matthew 11:28-29 – "Come to Me, all you who labor and are heavy laden, and I will give you rest. Take My yoke upon you and learn from Me, for I am gentle and lowly in heart, and you will find rest for your souls. For My yoke is easy and My burden is light."

Why do humans get sick? The cause is the fall. Also, sometimes it is the devil.

Faith is a key to flowing in the healing anointing.

Romans 10:17 – "Faith comes by hearing, and hearing by the word of God." Hearing, and hearing, and hearing, and hearing . . .

Hebrews 11:6 – "But without faith it is impossible to please Him, for he who comes to God must believe that He is, and that He is a rewarder of those who diligently seek Him."

2 Corinthians 4:13 – faith is a spirit…Faith is a someone, Jesus Christ.

Seven Reasons Jesus Healed

1.) Compassion – Mark 1:41- compassion has action; not sympathy

2.) Healing belongs to His children; it is the children's bread – Mark 7:27

3.) To glorify the Father – Matthew 15:30-31

4.) To fulfill the promises of God – Matt. 8:16-17

5.) To confirm His word – John 10:37-38 – miracles confirm the word. If you don't believe what I say, believe for the works sake. Let the works prove to you that what I am saying is God's word.

6.) Because of the blood covenant – Isaiah 53:4 – there is healing in the atonement

7.) To destroy the works of the devil – Acts 10:38

Isaiah 53:4 – "Surely He has borne our griefs, and carried our sorrows; yet we esteemed Him stricken, smitten by God, and afflicted."

The word "griefs" is Hebrew "kholee" which means "weaknesses, sicknesses, and afflictions."

"Sorrows" is the Hebrew "makob," meaning "our pain."

This covers everything!!
Jesus says "done, done, done."
Religion says "do, do, do."

Eight Reasons Why Believers Get Sick

1.) They will not confess their faults; If no confession, there may be sickness – James 5:16 – "confess faults to one another, that you may be healed"

Psalm 32 – "when I kept silent [no confession of sin], my bones waxed old [sickness]." He also dried up spiritually; when you confess your sin, God will send protection your way. His presence is restored to you; v. 7

2.) Because of idolatry; idols, idol worship – Exodus 32:35

The Lord plagued the people, because they made the calf.

Jesus said, "if you have anything against your bro, go to him." Otherwise, there is judgment.

"If you will not forgive, you will be given to the tormenters."

What is an idol? Anything or anyone that takes the place of God.

First commandment – "No other gods before Me."

3.) They persecute the righteous, God's servant

4.) They do not seek the Lord
2 Chronicles 16:10-12 – Asa persecuted the prophet
Praylessness is a sin
Samuel- I will not sin against the Lord by not praying for you.

5.) Rebellion
2 Chronicles 21:12 – King would not obey God or walk with God. The result was sickness on his children, wives, cattle, himself.

6.) Working too hard and long – Phil. 2:25

7.) Dishonor of parents/father and mother – Ephesians 6:2,3

God's best is divine health; healing is God's second best.
Psalm 105:37 – "there was not one feeble among all Israel"; when God brought them out of Egypt.

Psalm 103:3 – Who forgives all your iniquities, Who heals all your diseases . . .

8.) They forget God's promises, greatness, goodness, power, and more
Psalm 78:41-42 – powerful truth – they limited the Holy One of Israel
When you forget, you limit God.

Two Sins God Will Not Forgive
1.) Blasphemy of the Holy Spirit
2.) Unforgiveness

If you do return and seek Him, He will renew your youth like the eagle.

The Eagle and Healing

How an eagle operates reveals how someone can be healed instantly.

These scriptures contain glorious revelations.

Habakkuk 1:8 – "the eagle that hasteth to eat." The Christian who hastes, who can't wait, who hurries to eat God's word will find healing.

Job 39:27 – eagle lives on a rock, a high place. If we stand on the rock, Jesus Christ, healing will come. Stand on rock = reliance on God.

Proverbs 23:5 – eagle looks toward heaven. We must look upon Jesus.

Jeremiah 48:40 – eagle surrenders to the wind to fly. If we learn how to surrender to the Lord, healing will come.

Psalm 91:16 – He wants to prolong your youth.

Job 5:25-26 – if you obey the Lord, you will come to your grave at a full age, without sickness.

It's God's will that every believer be healed.

TWO

God's Will is Health & Healing

God's will is your health. Healing is His second best.

Hebrews 4:15 – He is touched and moved with our infirmities

Psalm 103 – God satisfies us with good things

The Father, Son, and Holy Spirit Agree:

Luke 13:16 – Jesus reaffirmed that sickness is "bondage" – the Son

Job 42:10 – called sickness "captivity" – the Father

Acts 10:38 – Holy Spirit called sickness "oppression" – the Holy Spirit

God Almighty has declared war on sin and sickness.

To receive healing, we must follow His instructions.

God has guaranteed your healing.

Proverbs 4:13 – "Take firm hold of instruction, do not let go; keep her, for she is your life."

Numbers 23:19 – "God is not a man that He should lie."

Psalm 89:17 – "For you are their glory and strength, and by your favor you exalt our horn. 18 Indeed, our shield belongs to the LORD, our king to the Holy One of Israel."

Strength – the word here is "healing," "health."

Our "horn" is our authority, because of who we are in Christ.

Because of God's glory, He wants to heal us.

Psalm 89:34 – "My covenant I shall not break" – God cannot break His word

Mark 7:13 – Jesus said the "word of God has become of no effect due to tradition" – powerful truth and revelation: instruction and the word are powerful, but if tradition is stronger than His instruction, the word will have no effect.

Jairus – Mark 5, Matthew 9:18 – he was ruler of synagogue. He broke tradition by kneeling before Jesus, which symbolized worship. And his daughter was healed.

Peter saw a vision of the animals. God had to rebuke him, "don't call unclean what I've cleansed." God was revealing that He would bring the gospel to the Gentiles.

Psalm 103 – God forgives. 1 John – we must confess before He forgives.

Someone may blaspheme the Holy Spirit through ignorance and be forgiven – Proof? Paul the Apostle. God's mercy.
Willful, knowing act of blasphemy of the Holy Spirit is a different matter.

Psalm 103:1-5 –
"Bless the Lord, O my soul;
And all that is within me, bless His holy name!
Bless the Lord, O my soul,
And forget not all His benefits:
Who forgives all your iniquities,
Who heals all your diseases,
Who redeems your life from destruction,
Who crowns you with lovingkindness and tender mercies,
Who satisfies your mouth with good things,
So that your youth is renewed like the eagle's."

The promises are yours IF you are obeying Him, living right.
How do you "bless the Lord"?
By serving Him. By glorifying Him through your actions, your service, your worship.

Three Glorious Keys:
1. Bless the Lord – by obeying Him, serving Him

2. Bless His name – His Name exalted. He must be first in your life.

3. Forget not His benefits and promises

Psalm 78:41,42 – they limited Him and remembered not His covenant

"crowns you" – puts a mantle on you, surrounds you, with lovingkindness and tender mercies.

Sozo – the Greek word for "salvation" – means full salvation, includes physical, spiritual, from everything from the enemy.

Healing is the salvation of Jesus Christ having its divine action in my body.

Exodus 15:26 – "For I am the LORD who heals you."

Exodus 15:25-26 – "There He made a statute and an ordinance for them, and there He tested them, and said, 'If you diligently heed the voice of the LORD your God and do what is right in His sight, give ear to His commandments and keep all His statutes, I will put none of the diseases on you which I have brought on the Egyptians. For I am the LORD who heals you.'"

1. Hear His voice; relationship with Him, fellowship
2. Obedience
3. Give ear – commit yourself to Him and His law
4. Keep all His statutes – Keep means "protect"

I will put none of the diseases on you – means they were already healed.

Psalm 105:37 – "He also brought them out with silver and gold, and there was none feeble among His tribes."
Not one feeble, sick, weak among you.
They left Egypt the same as eating the Passover, a type of accepting Christ as Savior, God healed three million people. They walked out a healed people.
If you walk out, you will also experience the same.
Egypt – symbolic of sin, the old life
In coming out, miracles waited for them.
If we stay in Egypt/sin, sickness may stay

Exodus 23:25 – "And I will take sickness away from the midst of you."

Exodus 23:25 – "So you shall serve the LORD your God, and He will bless your bread and your water. And I will take sickness away from the midst of you. No one shall suffer miscarriage or be barren in your land; I will fulfill the number of your days."

This is a powerful promise.

Deuteronomy 7:15 – "And the LORD will take away from you all sickness, and will afflict you with none of the terrible diseases of Egypt which you have known, but will lay them on all those who hate you."

Jesus came to save the soul and the body.

Ephesians 5:23 – "For the husband is head of the wife, as also Christ is head of the church; and He is the Savior of the body."

Jesus the savior of the body – double-meaning: the body of Christ, and the human body of individuals

We should resist sickness just like we resist sin.
Divine healing is good. Divine health is better.

Isaiah 53 –
"Who has believed our report?
And to whom has the arm of the LORD been revealed?
2 For He shall grow up before Him as a tender plant,
And as a root out of dry ground.
He has no form or comeliness;
And when we see Him,
There is no beauty that we should desire Him.
3 He is despised and rejected by men,

A Man of sorrows and acquainted with grief.
And we hid, as it were, our faces from Him;
He was despised, and we did not esteem Him.
4 Surely He has borne our griefs
And carried our sorrows;
Yet we esteemed Him stricken,
Smitten by God, and afflicted.
5 **But He was wounded for our transgressions,**

He was bruised for our iniquities;

The chastisement for our peace was upon Him,

And by His stripes we are healed.
6 All we like sheep have gone astray;
We have turned, every one, to his own way;
And the LORD has laid on Him the iniquity of us all.
7 He was oppressed and He was afflicted,
Yout He opened not His mouth;
He was led as a lamb to the slaughter,
And as a sheep before its shearers is silent,
So He opened not His mouth.
8 He was taken from prison and from judgment,
And who will declare His generation?
For He was cut off from the land of the living;
For the transgressions of My people He was stricken.
9 And they made His grave with the wicked—
But with the rich at His death,
Because He had done no violence,
Nor was any deceit in His mouth.

10 Yet it pleased the LORD to bruise Him;
He has put Him to grief.
When You make His soul an offering for sin,
He shall see His seed, He shall prolong His days,
And the pleasure of the LORD shall prosper in His hand.
11 He shall see the labor of His soul,[b] and be satisfied.
By His knowledge My righteous Servant shall justify many,
For He shall bear their iniquities.
12 Therefore I will divide Him a portion with the great,
And He shall divide the spoil with the strong,
Because He poured out His soul to death,
And He was numbered with the transgressors,
And He bore the sin of many,
And made intercession for the transgressors."

He was wounded
Bruised
Chastised
By His "stripes" – bruises, wounds
Blood was shed for sin. Blood makes atonement for the soul.
Body was broken for healing.
Let's accept both
Triple-cure
Our spirit is renewed.
Our soul is saved.
Our body is healed.

Job 33:24, 25 – "Then He is gracious to him, and says, 'Deliver him from going down to the Pit; I have found a ransom'; His flesh shall be young like a child's, He shall return to the days of his youth."

THREE

Triple Cure for Man, a Three-fold Being

Man is a three-fold being. Man is a spirit, who has a soul, and lives in a body.

1 Thessalonians 5:23 – "Now may the God of peace Himself sanctify you completely; and may your whole spirit, soul, and body be preserved blameless at the coming of our Lord Jesus Christ."

The fall: the spirit died; soul became burdened with sorrow; body became subject to sickness and disease.

James 1:18 – we as believers are "begotten" children not created children. Adam was created a child of God. Begotten means we are in a higher plane that unfallen man, than Adam was even in his perfect state.

Adam was not born of the Spirit. He did not have a recreated human spirit. He was not born again. He was created.

Begotten means the Holy Spirit breathed His life into your spirit. His nature became a part of your nature. Your spirit and the Lord's Spirit became one. We are one with Him.

Jesus said, "I in them, they in Me."

1 Corinthians 6:17 – "But he who is joined to the Lord is one spirit with Him."

He that is joined to the Lord is one spirit with Him.

Oneness beyond explanation.

You and Jesus became united, no separation. It's beyond union and oneness. You cannot separate the Lord from the church or vice-versa. He is the head, we are the body.

Ephesians 1 – When God spoke it, He established it forever. Summary of Ephesians 1:

I was chosen before the foundation of the world

I am holy – I am blameless – I am adopted – I am accepted – I am redeemed – I have all wisdom – I know His will – I have an inheritance – I am sealed with the Holy Spirit of promise

Romans 8:29 – "Our spirit man is being conformed to the image of Christ. Our spirit man is justified and glorified."

Our spirit man is healed and healyour.

Triple Cure – Spirit, Soul, Body

God offers healing of all three of man's parts: spirit, soul, and body. Let's first look at:
Isaiah 53:5-6 – "But He was wounded for our transgressions,
He was bruised for our iniquities;
The chastisement for our peace was upon Him,
And by His stripes we are healed.
All we like sheep have gone astray;
We have turned, every one, to his own way;
And the LORD has laid on Him the iniquity of us all. "

In God's awesome, glorious proclamation to Moses recorded in Exodus 34, God declares that He forgives "iniquity and transgression and sin."
Exodus 34:6-7 – "And the Lord passed before him and proclaimed, 'The Lord, the Lord God, merciful and gracious, longsuffering, and abounding in goodness and truth, keeping mercy for thousands, forgiving iniquity and transgression and sin . . .'"
There is a great mystery here, but let's focus on the fact that God forgives and heals man fully and completely, in all three parts.
Man is a fallen being. Transgression is birthed in the spirit; iniquity is birthed in the soul; sin is active in the body.

Spirit:
Isaiah 53:5 – "He was wounded for our transgressions."

Proverbs 18:14 – it is the spirit that gets wounded.

His spirit was wounded when God left Him on the cross: "Father, why have You forsaken Me?"

Soul:
Jesus was bruised for our iniquities.

"My soul is exceedingly sorrowful" – Matthew 26:34

Christ became sin; His soul was bruised when our sins became His.

He was chastised for our peace.

Triple Cure for Man: Spirit, Soul, Body		
Transgression	Spirit	Birth of sin
Iniquity	Soul	Decision of sin
Sin	Body	Act of sin

Body:
Deuteronomy 28 – lists 39 diseases

The old law of whipping was 39 lashes.

Paul was whipped 40 times minus one.

So we can really say, "With His stripes we are healed." All diseases. Spirit is the real me.

Soul is my emotions, personality, and intellect.

My body is the house.

FOUR

Jesus & the Passover: Healing

The result of the cross is healing.

Whenever Israel honored the blood covenant, healing came.

When Israel ate the passover, the result was healing.

1 Corinthians 11:23-26 – "For I received from the Lord that which I also delivered to you: that the Lord Jesus on the same night in which He was betrayed took bread; and when He had given thanks, He broke it and said, 'Take, eat; this is My body which is broken for you; do this in remembrance of Me.' In the same manner He also took the cup after supper, saying, 'This cup is the new covenant in My blood. This do, as often as you drink it, in remembrance of Me.'

For as often as you eat this bread and drink this cup, you proclaim the Lord's death till He comes."

We must not forget the covenant. It is absolutely powerful.
v. 23 – the Lord gave Paul this truth

Exodus 12:3-11
"Speak to all the congregation of Israel, saying: 'On the tenth of this month every man shall take for himself a lamb, according to the house of his father, a lamb for a household. 4 And if the household is too small for the lamb, let him and his neighbor next to his house take it according to the number of the persons; according to each man's need you shall make your count for the lamb. 5 Your lamb shall be without blemish, a male of the first year. You may take it from the sheep or from the goats. 6 Now you shall keep it until the fourteenth day of the same month. Then the whole assembly of the congregation of Israel shall kill it at twilight. 7 And they shall take some of the blood and put it on the two door posts and on the lintel of the houses where they eat it. 8 Then they shall eat the flesh on that night; roasted in fire, with unleavened bread and with bitter herbs they shall eat it. 9 Do not eat it raw, nor boiled at all with water, but roasted in fire—its head with its legs and its entrails. 10 You shall let none of it remain until morning, and what remains of it until morning you shall

burn with fire. 11 And thus you shall eat it: with a belt on your waist, your sandals on your feet, and your staff in your hand. So you shall eat it in haste. It is the LORD's Passover.'"

Old Covenant is the shadow
New Covenant is the substance

The glorious truths of the new life in Jesus are revealed in both the Old and New Covenants, or Testaments. The Old Covenant is the shadow, or type and symbol, of the truths. In the New Covenant, the truths are fulfilled and are therefore the substance.

Explanation of the Passover

v. 3 – A lamb for a house – God believes in household salvation – if one person is saved in a family, there is an umbrella of salvation for them all.

v. 6 – 14th day – evening –

fire, unleavened bread, bitter herbs, nothing left until the morning

v. 11 – loins girded, eat in haste – They were healed as they were eating and leaving.

Every time you partake communion, you partake of Christ.

There is healing in the atonement.

Hebrews 9:11-12 – "But Christ came as High Priest of the good things to come, with the greater and more perfect tabernacle not made with hands, that is, not of this creation. Not with the blood of goats and calves, but with His own blood He entered the Most Holy Place once for all, having obtained eternal redemption."

The blood of Jesus will set you free from your past.

v. 19 – "For when Moses had spoken every precept to all the people according to the law, he took the blood of calves and goats, with water, scarlet wool, and hyssop, and sprinkled both the book itself and all the people."

Moses took blood of calves, goats, with:

water – the word

scarlet – the suffering of Christ

wool – His judgment

hyssop – a plant used to spray the blood – symbolic of faith

sprinkled the book

Psalm 51:7 – "Purge me with hyssop, and I shall be clean; wash me, and I shall be whiter than snow."

"purge me with hyssop and I shall be clean..."

"This is the blood of the Testament"

Because of the blood, everything is ours. We should lack nothing because of the blood.

Faith is the result of the revelation of the blood covenant. Revelation of the cross will birth faith.

James 1:6-7 – "But let him ask in faith, with no doubting, for he who doubts is like a wave of the sea driven and tossed by the wind. For let not that man suppose that he will receive anything from the Lord; 8 he is a double-minded man, unstable in all his ways."

"let him ask in faith…"

2 Peter 1:3-4 – "as His divine power has given to us all things that pertain to life and godliness, through the knowledge of Him who called us by glory and virtue, by which have been given to us exceedingly great and precious promises, that through these you may be partakers of the divine nature, having escaped the corruption that is in the world through lust."

"All things" in this life and Godliness

1 John 3:21-22 – "Beloved, if our heart does not condemn us, we have confidence toward God. And whatever we ask we receive from Him, because we keep His commandments and do those things that are pleasing in His sight."

If we are living right, our hearts will not condemn us. Then there is confidence toward God, there is faith.

Holy living produces faith. If someone is in sin, they do not have confidence or faith toward God.

FIVE

How to Receive Healing and Divine Health

To receive divine health:
One – Abide in Him- John 15:7
Two – Let the word work its healing power in you
Three – John 5 – Will you be made whole? Man with infirmity for 38 years healed at Pool of Bethesda – Find someone who will believe with you.

Abide in Him- John 15:7
1 John 3:6 – "Whoever abides in Him does not sin. Whoever sins has neither seen Him nor known Him."
We must cooperate with Him – John 8:31-32 - "Then Jesus said to those Jews who believed

Him, 'If you abide in My word, you are My disciples indeed. And you shall know the truth, and the truth shall make you free.'" John 8:31-32

How to receive healing

One – Receive the word of healing
Psalm 107:20 – He sent his word and healed them
Two – Let the wrd work its healing pwr in you
1 Thessalonians 2:13 – word works effectually in them that believe
Three – John 5 – will you be made whole – Find someone who will believe with you.
Psalm 89:34 – his word is established forever.

Why is that unbelievers sometimes get healed quickly, while sometimes believers may not be healed as fast?

T.L. Osborne – "Because the unbeliever gets healed because of God's mercy, while the believer gets healed because of God's covenant. However, unbelievers are the ones who lose their healing."

Believers are under an entire different system. Imagine two rooms: "Mercy room" and "Covenant room." Believers have to go to the Covenant room and learn about it before they can receive their healing.

People lose their healing because there is no foundation. The covenant is part of that foundation.

The first covenant God made with Israel after they left Egypt: the covenant of healing.

Healing in Book of Numbers, fulfilled in Jesus Christ

Numbers 21:8-9 – "Then the Lord said to Moses, '**Make a fiery serpent, and set it on a pole; and it shall be that everyone who is bitten, when he looks at it, shall live.**' So Moses made a bronze serpent, and put it on a pole; and so it was, if a serpent had bitten anyone, when he looked at the bronze serpent, he lived."

Israel came to the wilderness. Many were bitten by serpents, got sick and died. Moses cried out to the Lord. The Lord said take this pole, put a serpent on it, and whoever looks at the serpent will be healed. The serpent is symbolic of Christ on the cross.

In John 3, Jesus said: "'And as Moses lifted up the serpent in the wilderness, even so must the Son of Man be lifted up, that whoever believes in Him should not perish but have eternal life.'" John 3:14-15

Key to miracles: a continual look by faith at Jesus Christ. The healing process begins and goes on while I look at Christ. Looking by faith.

Look – to receive; to be clothed with; to be overcome by; to be enraptured in. Look means a present experience. The One I see will clothe me. I will walk in Him, and He will walk in me. Look means a union of the two coming together.

You are no longer aware of yourself, your sickness, your pain, or anyone else. You become aware of Him and totally conscious of Him.

Preparation is: the word building faith in you. It enables you to draw near to Him.

Jeremiah 33:3 – "Call to Me, and I will answer you, and show you great and mighty things, which you do not know."

It begins with calling Him, knocking. And visiting His presence.

He answers. He shows you Himself, great and mighty things which you do not know. That happens when you touch Him with your faith. Your faith is lifted as the word pours within you. Worship enables the spirit to release what's within. Every time you worship, the soul and body are laid aside, and the spirit comes into action. There is a release of the river Jesus talked about. Living water touches your soul.

Worship is in the innermost holy sanctuary.

Tabernacle's Three Sections: Three Parts of Man		
Outer Court	Body	Confession
Holy Place	Soul	Praise
Holy of Holies	Spirit	Intimacy

Confession – cleansed by the blood
The greatest worship is in silence – Job 5

SIX

Jesus: God's Will in Action

Jesus Christ is God. He is Jehovah.

If you want to know what God is like, look at Jesus Christ.

Jesus is the will of God in action.

The Trinity is One.

John 14:9-11 – "Jesus said to him, 'Have I been with you so long, and yet you have not known Me, Philip? He who has seen Me has seen the Father; so how can you say, 'Show us the Father'? Do you not believe that I am in the Father, and the Father in Me? The words that I speak to you I do not speak on My own authority; but the Father who dwells in Me does the works. Believe Me that I am in the Father and the Father in Me, or else believe Me for the sake of the works themselves.'"

Acts 10:38 – "how God anointed Jesus of Nazareth with the Holy Spirit and with power, who went about doing good and healing all who were oppressed by the devil, for God was with Him."

Psalm 34:8 – "O taste and see that the Lord is good."

God made the earth and its fullness. He made man, and gave man dominion over all things on the earth.

Genesis 1:26 – "Then God said, 'Let Us make man in Our image, according to Our likeness; let them have dominion over the fish of the sea, over the birds of the air, and over the cattle, over all the earth and over every creeping thing that creeps on the earth.'"

God owns the earth but does not dominate it. He gave the dominion of the earth to Adam, to man. It's like someone building a house, paying for all of it, and giving it to someone else to live in and have dominion over. God is still the owner of the earth.

Psalm 89:11 – "The heavens are Yours, the earth also is Yours; the world and all its fullness, You have founded them."

Adam lost that dominion. The serpent deceived the woman, who ate the fruit, then gave the fruit to Adam, who ate. Adam lost his authority when he sinned.

Adam had the legal right to give the earth to

whoever he wanted. In Luke 4:5-8, Satan tempted Jesus by saying "all the kingdoms of the world are my" and offering them to Jesus. Satan actually told the truth in this scripture. When Adam gave Satan dominion over the earth, Satan became the god of this world. Today, Satan still has authority and dominion over the earth.

2 Corinthians 4:4 – Satan is the "god of this world."

Ephesians 2:2 – Satan is called the "prince of the power of the air."

John 12:31; John 14:30; John 16:11 – Jesus called Satan the "prince of this world" three times.

Satan is still today the god and prince of this world.

Revelation 11:15 – "Then the seventh angel sounded: And there were loud voices in heaven, saying, 'The kingdoms of this world have become the kingdoms of our Lord and of His Christ, and He shall reign forever and ever!'"

The day is coming when the world will return to its Owner. He will again have the authority over it. The earth is still the Lord's today, but THE WORLD is under the dominion of Satan.

"The earth is the Lord's, and all its fullness [everything in it] . ." (Psalm 24:1a).

Revelation 12:10 – "Then I heard a loud voice saying in heaven, 'Now salvation, and strength, and the kingdom of our God, and the power of His Christ have come, for the accuser of our brethren, who accused them before our God day and night, has been cast down.'"

All that happens on the earth is happening and has happened because of the fall. God is not behind it. God opposes it.

What is behind it? Sin. The fall of man. Behind all that, is Satan.

In our world, the natural disasters are often called "Acts of God." They are not acts of God. They are the result of the fall. Satan is ruling the world and has dominion over the earth. Therefore, any evil and sickness is from him.

Sickness is not of God. It cannot be.

The body breaks down. There is sickness. We sin. But there is forgiveness.

Even Elisha, anointed man of God, died "a sick man."

Job 1 – They say "God allowed sickness."

They ask "Why doesn't God intervene?"

What happened to Job?

God protected Job, because Job was a man of prayer. He was righteous. The earth was already under Satan's dominion.

Satan was given permission to do what he has always done, but it is not talked about. Satan has always been a murderer.

God intervened and protected Job, just like He has done with His people who are people of prayer and righteousness.

God is a healing God. Sickness cannot come from God.

Prayer and only prayer brings God's intervention.

Job: God gave Satan permission to send calamity to Job.

Job lost everything in one day. Later God restored all that Job lost—and double; because Job was faithful.

Satan accused Job and did all the evil.

That is why we need a High Priest, interceding for us before God's throne.

Revelation 7:25 – "Therefore He is also able to save to the uttermost those who come to God through Him, since He always lives to make intercession for them."

He intercedes to keep up saved and free.

When Job was accused, there was no mediator. There was not someone like Christ. There is a mystery here.

We need Him forever? Yes.

It was not God's will that harm came to Job. It was Satan's will.

Acts 10:38 – He healed all oppressed of the devil.

Sickness is not from God. Does a father on earth ever want sickness on their children?

Sickness is an oppression of the devil. Satan is behind it. It does not always mean there is a demon involved.

Jesus healed "all."

Mark 16:15-18 – Jesus authorizes His followers to "lay hands on the sick."

"And Jesus said to them, 'Go into all the world

and preach the gospel to every creature. He who believes and is baptized will be saved; but he who does not believe will be condemned. And these signs will follow those who believe: In My name they will cast out demons; they will speak with new tongues; they will take up serpents; and if they drink anything deadly, it will by no means hurt them; they will lay hands on the sick, and they will recover.'"

All believers have authority to lay hands on the sick.

James 5:14-15 – "Is anyone among you sick? Let him call for the elders of the church, and let them pray over him, anointing him with oil in the name of the Lord. And the prayer of faith will save the sick, and the Lord will raise him up. And if he has committed sins, he will be forgiven."

Prayer of faith – There are no "if's" in the kingdom of God. It's "yes and amen."

The Number of Your Days – we are promised 70 years, possibly 80 years.
Psalm 90:10 – "The days of our lives are seventy years; And if by reason of strength they are eighty years, yet their boast is only labor and sorrow; For it is soon cut off, and we fly away."

God has made full provision. We have to re-

ceive it.
Salvation is a provision. We have to receive it.

There are many promises of health in the Bible. He is for righteousness and health.

Deuteronomy 7:11 – "I want you to be righteous. His will is righteousness in your life."
v. 15 – The Lord will take away all sickness. It is His will.

Jesus is God's will in action. If you want to see God, if you want to know what God is like, look at Jesus. One day, the authority of this planet will return to its owner: Jesus Christ.

Healing is part of God's redemptive plan.
God is the author of all that is good. Satan is the author of all that is evil.
Where did sin come from? The heart of Lucifer, an archangel.

Ezekiel 28:15 – "You were perfect in your ways from the day you were created, till iniquity was found in you."
This sin brought about sickness to humanity. Eve became obedient to the author of sin. She became his property. She was no longer under God's authority. Adam and Eve switched masters.
Jesus could have sinned. Why would the Holy

Spirit lead Him to be tempted if he could not have sinned?

He was tempted in all points. He learned obedience. He was as much man, as though he was not God. He was as much God as though he was not man. He is the perfect God and perfect man in one. He is all God and all man. He was God in flesh.

For we do not have a High Priest who cannot sympathize with our weaknesses, but was in all points tempted as we are, yet without sin.

Through His perfection, He won the victory. He became our substitute. He defeated the purpose of Satan. He destroyed the works of the devil.

1 John 3:8 – "He who sins is of the devil, for the devil has sinned from the beginning. For this purpose the Son of God was manifested, that He might destroy the works of the devil."

Jesus came to heal. Satan came to "steal, kill and destroy."

SEVEN

The Full Gospel: Forgiveness and Healing

Forgiveness and healing are twins. They are closely related.

Sin and sickness are twins. They also are closely related.

Matthew 8:16-18 – "When evening had come, they brought to Him many who were demon-possessed. And He cast out the spirits with a word, and healed all who were sick, that it might be fulfilled which was spoken by Isaiah the prophet, saying: 'He Himself took our infirmities, and bore our sicknesses.'"

Matthew 9:6 – "'But that you may know that the Son of Man has power on earth to forgive sins' – then He said to the paralytic, 'Arise, take up your bed, and go to your house.'"

We are a combination of spirit and soul/flesh, heaven and earth.
Soul gets sinful. Body gets sick.
Sin exists in the soul. Sickness exists in the body.

Isaiah 33:24 - "And the inhabitant will not say, 'I am sick'; the people who dwell in it will be forgiven their iniquity."
Jesus fulfilled this scripture. He forgave and healed.

Matthew 4:23 – "healing all manner of sickness and disease."
Hebrews 13:8 – "Jesus Christ is the same yesterday, today, and forever."
Matthew 11:5 – "Jesus answered and said to them, 'Go and tell John the things which you hear and see: The blind see and the lame walk; the lepers are cleansed and the deaf hear; the dead are raised up and the poor have the gospel preached to them.'"

The prophets predicted the Messiah would both forgive and heal. When we deny that he heals, we take away his title as Messiah. If we say he only saves, we take away his title. It's the full gospel.

Mark 2 – Jesus tells a man, "your sins are forgiven." Jesus reveals in these statements that it is easier to forgive than it is to heal a paralytic. The people were amazed. How dare we take away from Him what belongs to Him, by saying He doesn't heal anymore.

Forgiveness of sin and healing of the body complete each other.
Sin and sickness are as united as soul and body; not soul and spirit.
The body is the house. The soul is the personality, intellect, will, and emotions.
When someone is forgiven but not healed, they have not received the fullness of redemption, the fruit of redemption. When healed, it is complete.

Sometimes Jesus healed first which prepared the way for forgiveness, such as Matthew 11:5.
In Mt 9:6 – He forgave first and then He healed.
Healing seals the work. It is complete.
Redemption is a process.
"My spirit was saved. My soul is being saved and renewed day by day. My body will be saved."

Acts 3:16 – "And His name, through faith in His name, has made this man strong, whom you see and know. Yous, the faith which comes through Him has given him this perfect soundness in the presence of you all."
Perfect soundness = healing

Acts 4:10 – the name of Jesus heals and saves.

Romans 8:22-23 - "For we know that the whole creation groans and labors with birth pangs together until now. Not only that, but we also who have the firstfruits of the Spirit, even we ourselves groan within ourselves, eagerly waiting for the adoption, the redemption of our body."

Our body will experience full redemption one day. Provision is here for healing. One day, corruption will put on incorruption.

Many have rejected healing because there are other ways to be healed. There is only one way to be saved. The blessing of healing brings intimacy with Jesus Christ, so these people are missing out on the benefits of healing.

Faith and Healing

As you have believed, so let it be done for you . . .

Matthew 8:13 - "Then Jesus said to the centurion, 'Go your way; and as you have believed, so let it be done for you.'"

This is a principal law of God's kingdom. He gives in proportion to our faith. He gives or withholds his grace according to faith.

Faith is born of the Holy Spirit. If the Spirit is present, faith is present. When the Spirit is present, prayer is present. He is the Spirit of prayer and faith. That power will give you power to pray, to believe God's word, to live the Christian life in its fullness, to be victorious.

Faith is not produced by the mind.

It is our job to cooperate. You cooperate when you believe. You believe when you live it and act it. The presence of God is there. He commands us to speak, to say it.

God leads. He does not push. We follow. We walk with Him. We have to cooperate. Faith is released when we cooperate with Him. Action releases faith.

James 1:5-8

Matthew 17:20 – "So Jesus said to them, 'Because of your unbelief; for assuredly, I say to you, if you have faith as a mustard seed, you will say to this mountain, 'Move from here to there,' and it will move; and nothing will be impossible for you.'"

Ephesians 2:8 – "For by grace you have been saved through faith, and that not of yourselves; it is the gift of God, 9 not of works, lest anyone should boast."

Only through faith can we receive healing.

James 5:15

Matthew 21:22 – "'And whatever things you ask in prayer, believing, you will receive.'"

EIGHT

Healing in the Old Covenant

The fruit of salvation and redemption is healing.

Hebrews 10:23 – "Let us hold fast the confession of our hope without wavering, for He who promised is faithful."

John 5:6 – "'Will you be made whole?'"

James 4:2– "You have not because you ask not." God healed those who asked him and requested healing.

Is healing in the atonement?

Some will say that Isaiah 53 is purely spiritual.

Romans 5:12 - "Therefore, just as through one man sin entered the world, and death through sin, and thus death spread to all men, because all sinned . . ."

The remedy for sin is found in the cross.

The remedy for healing and disease is found also in the cross.

Since disease is a part of the curse, it is true remedy must be the cross.

Old Covenant was the shadow, Jesus is the substance.

There are types in the Old Covenant for everything we walk in. We have the substance. The Old Covenant was a shadow. Jesus is in every book. The Bible is a revelation of Jesus.

Exodus 12

God offers salvation to every man in Israel.

If there are not enough people, bring your neighbors in.

Lamb without blemish = Jesus

Kill it in the evening = Jesus

The door posts = the cross

They shall eat it = eating of the lamb took place after the application of the blood.

Fire

Unleavened bread

Bitter herbs

They applied the blood, then they ate the lamb. They ate the lamb for strength, for the journey. More than that, it is a type.

Psalm 105:37 – There was not one feeble among their tribes.

They left after receiving health.

Were they healed in Egypt? No.

Exodus 15 – "I will put none of these diseases upon you which I have brought upon the Egyptians. Sickness struck in Egypt."

Exodus 23:25 – "I will take sickness away from the midst of you."

Deuteronomy 7:15 – "The Lord will take away all sickness and will put none of the evil diseases which you knew . . ." = They knew what sickness was. They experienced sickness prior to Exodus 12. God calls sickness "evil."

1 Corinthians 5:7 – Jesus is our Passover.

They received healing after they ate the Passover.

2 Chronicles 30:20 – "And the LORD heard Hezekiah and healed the people."

Sickness had returned to Israel. Hezekiah celebrates Passover again. The result is the healing of the whole nation. They had not celebrated the Passover for hundreds of years.

God cannot break His word.

Healing is in the atonement mentioned repeatedly in Bible. When we see the cross, we see healing, both in Old and New Testament.

Exodus 15:23 – God showed Moses a tree, a type/symbol/shadow of the cross. Take a tree and cast it into the waters. Then and only then did God reveal Himself as Jehovah Rapha, the Lord Who Heals.

Exodus 12 – the blood applied, then lamb eaten and healing came.

Numbers 16 – the story of Korah; the earth swallowed Korah. Later the people opposed Moses again. A plague begins, and 14,000+ people died. Why did it stop? Moses told Aaron to take the censer and make an atonement now! Aaron runs through the camp with the censer, making atonement.

The Cross Brings Healing
When the Cross is Revealed, Healing Follows

Exodus 15:23 – the tree in the waters = the cross

Numbers 16:46-50 – the plague struck Israel – make an atonement for the people – when the cross was introduced to Israel, the plague was stopped, by which time 14,700 men, women, and children were slain by the disease. The cross stopped it.

God healed the people by introducing the cross to Israel.

After sin of Korah, the slaying of the 250, sickness re-entered as a result of rebellion.

Moses said to Aaron, take the censer and make

an atonement now for the people. He stood between the living and the dead, and the plague stopped.

Numbers 21 – Sin entered the camp. Serpents bit the people, sickness invaded the camp, and death and destruction came. Moses cried to the Lord. The Lord said, place a bronze serpent on a pole, and whoever looks upon that serpent shall live. This was a type and symbol of the cross.
Christ became sin on the cross.

David – Psalm 103 – "He heals all diseases, He forgives all iniquities."

Job 33:24 – the oldest book in the Bible.
When Job was struck with sickness and disease by the devil, when he was covered with boils, he discovered the ransom, the work of the cross.

This is the key, the secret. Every time the cross is revealed, healing follows. If we bring the cross back in our lives, healing will touch our bodies. The cross will drive disease out of your body.

Jeremiah 17 – "Save me Lord and I shall be saved. Heal me and I shall be healed." He saw the cross and cried, "Heal me."

The Passover – when Israel partook of the lamb, it was a shadow of the cross and it healed them. They were healed through the shadow. We then must be healed, for we have the substance. If the shadow healed them, the substance will surely heal us.

1 Corinthians 11:30 – "For this cause many are weak and sickly among you."

v. 29 – "He that eats and drinks unworthily, eats and drinks damnation to himself, not discerning the Lord's body." This deals with communion.

The reason many are sick is that we have lost the "union of Jesus" in communion. We have taken Christ out of the communion. If we bring Christ back and have union with Him in our communion with Him, we shall and must be healed.

The blood was shed for your redemption.

The body was broken for your health.

NINE

Objections and Roadblocks to Healing

There are numerous objections and roadblocks to healing. This chapter will cover eight (8) objections and additional roadblocks and hindrances, to healing. The eight objections are:

1. Sickness comes to purify me.
2. Healing is not God's will.
3. Some Old & New Testament saints were sick.
4. Paul had a thorn in his flesh.
5. Sickness is suffering with Jesus.
6. God allows sickness to discipline His children.
7. God allows sickness so His children can be holy.
8. I'm suffering for the glory of God.

Objection One:
Sickness comes to purify me

Ecclesiastes 3:1 – "There is a time for everything . . . a time to kill, a time to heal."

Solomon is writing about life. See Ecclesiastes 1:9. He is not writing that God is giving us permission to kill. God is not giving us permission to tear down. In life, both good and bad things happen.

Ecclesiastes 1:9 – "That which has been is what will be, that which is done is what will be done, and there is nothing new under the sun."

This passage does not say that God causes these bad things to happen.

In fact, every good and perfect gift comes down from the Father of lights. There is no evil in Him.

Objection Two:
Healing is not God's will

Their scripture: Isaiah 45:7 – "I form the light and create darkness, I make peace and create calamity; I, the LORD, do all these things."

We must look at the whole Bible. The Bible interprets the Bible.

Jesus Christ is God's will in action.

Isaiah 42:3 says, "Even the wick of a candle he will not quench."

To know God, look at Jesus. Everything Jesus did is God's will in action. Jesus healed. That's

God's will in action.
He saved.
He rescued.
He forgave the sinner.
He loved the lost.
He cast out demons.
All of that is God's will in action.
Jesus Christ is God's will in action.

Acts 10:38 – "He went about healing all oppressed of the devil."

In the Old Testament, God forgave and forgave. After hundreds of years, he still reaches out to a people who rebel and are hard-hearted, and say, "We don't want you. We will worship Baal..."

We must look at the full Bible and not take one scripture as truth.

God did not will for Israel to go to Babylon. He sent prophet after prophet. The people were so stubborn they said, "No, no, no..."

God is just and holy. Even though he is longsuffering, and was with Israel even after they rebelled and turned away from Him.

We should look at how he dealt with the nation Israel. Paul wrote, "It is written for our example." They came out of Egypt, and within a few days, they wondered about Moses, and said, "Let's forget this God and build a calf. We'll call it Jehovah and worship it." Aaron even said, "Yeah, you're right..." God in anger wants to destroy them. One man pleads for him not to. God repents because of one man. It was God's will for those people to make the promised land. In the wilderness, their rebellion reached such a height, he looked away. He took his hand away. God does not allow it. He just removes his hand of blessing and protection. God simply let go. They died in the wilderness.

In the Book of Jeremiah, in Babylon, the same thing happened. God kept coming back and giving them another chance. They rejected his offer, "We don't want that . . . We will worship devils," and they even wanted to kill him.

God did not allow it. The decision was theirs. They wanted to go to Egypt. He sends the spies, who say there are giants there. God in anger says "I give up!" He let them do what they want. It is not his nature to "drag" them into the promised land. He says, "Follow me." We choose to or not to.

He says, "Search for me…" It is His nature. We must pursue him and the will of God and the Lord.

The flesh hates everything that has to do with God's holiness and perfection. The flesh is looking back, like Lot's wife. We must take control of the flesh. We must fight it. Why? Because the flesh wants its own way. The flesh is fallen and falling. It wants to go into the pit.

The perfect will of God is secret. Deuteronomy 29:29 is below. It is preordained and determined.

The permissive will is revealed in the word of God.

Deuteronomy 29:29 – "The secret things belong to the LORD our God, but those things which are revealed belong to us and to our children forever, that we may do all the words of this law."

Daniel said there are things that are secret.

Daniel 2:22 – "He reveals deep and secret things; He knows what is in the darkness, And light dwells with Him."

Examples of his revealed will:

The revealed will – God is not willing that any should perish.

Lamentations 3:32-33 – "For He does not afflict willingly, nor grieve the children of men." It is not His will to afflict.

We should pursue the revealed will of God.

Jeremiah 33:19-20 – they put idols in the holy of holies. Yet God said "I am not breaking my covenant." That's a God whose longsuffering is beyond comprehension. You can put idols in the holy of holies, but He says, "I am not breaking My covenant. You can turn against Me, and hate Me, I will not turn against you or hate you." He is the God who is always reaching out.

Isaiah – "My hands are stretched out still."

To know what God is like, look at Jesus and what he did. Jesus continually did good, helped those in need.

It is his will to heal just as it is his will to save.

Psalm 25:8; Acts 10:38; Psalm 103; Isaiah 53:4; Jeremiah 30:17; 1 Peter 2:24; Romans 2:11; Matthew 8:1-3; 3 John 2; 1 John 5:14.

Objection Three:
Some Old & New Testament saints were sick

Elisha – 2 Kings 13,14 - he was old and died of old age. Sickness came in because of old age

Philippians 2:25-30 – Epaphraditis got sick. He worked too hard.

2 Timothy 4:20 – Trophimus got sick.

They would not take care of their body. We must take care of our body.

Objection Four:
Paul had a thorn in his flesh

2 Corinthians 12:7-10 – thorn in the flesh came as a result of heavenly revelations, spiritual experiences with God. Repeated blows and buffeting. It actually was not sickness.

If sickness is the result of heavenly revelations, then anyone who has heard God's voice should be sick.

God wanted to keep Paul humble. He sent a messenger of Satan to harass him with attacks, blow after blow.

Many men of God end up falling, because they had so much power, so much revelation. They began to believe things that were crazy.

Alexander Dowie had one of the greatest healing ministries in American history. He built the town Zion Illinois. In the end, he thought he was Elijah.

The Jeffrey brothers. In the end, they taught

heresy.

William Branham in the end thought he was Elijah.

The healing ministry includes people who went off course.

Objection Five:
Sickness is suffering with Jesus

Exodus 23:25-27 - "Yous, and all who desire to live godly in Christ Jesus will suffer persecution."

2 Timothy 2:12 – "If we endure, We shall also reign with Him. If we deny Him, He also will deny us."

Galatians 5:11 – why do I suffer persecutions

Philippians 1:29 – suffer for His sake

2 Timothy 3:12 – Yous, and all who desire to live godly in Christ Jesus will suffer persecution.

These were persecutions, not sickness.

Objection Six:
God allows sickness to discipline His children

Hebrews 12:6 – "Whom He loves, He chastises." Chastise means to educate, not punish with sickness.

Objection Seven:
God allows sickness so
His children can be holy

Healing is God's provision
If God sends sickness, why does He heal it?
It makes no sense to say that "God sends or allows sickness."

Objection Eight:
I'm suffering for the glory of God

The glory of God was revealed when Jesus healed people. The healing of the blind man and the resurrection of Lazarus were for the glory of God. The sickness was not for the glory of God.

Today, it brings God glory when people are healed.

John 11

Mental roadblocks

Is healing in the atonement? Yes.

Romans 5:12 – Therefore, just as through one man sin entered the world, and death through sin, and thus death spread to all men, because all sinned

Sickness entered into the world by sin. Its remedy is the redemption by Jesus Christ.

Where did sickness come from? Sickness comes from the fall of man. It's a process of death in the body.

2 Corinthians 4:10,11 – "Always carrying about in the body the dying of the Lord Jesus, that the life of Jesus also may be manifested in our body. 11 For we who live are always delivered

to death for Jesus' sake, that the life of Jesus also may be manifested in our mortal flesh."

Disease is a part of the curse. Therefore, it's remedy is the cross.

Everyone sins, because we are sinful by nature. If sin can touch my body, so can disease. Provision is there for healing.

Job 33:14-18 – Summary: God speaks once, twice, but man does not listen. Then He speaks while man slumbers. He is trying to save you from the pit. Once the man listened, God introduced a ransom, which brought healing. Man found favor.

Job 33:14-18, 24-26: "For God may speak in one way, or in another, yet man does not perceive it. In a dream, in a vision of the night, when deep sleep falls upon men, while slumbering on their beds, then He opens the ears of men, and seals their instruction. In order to turn man from his deed, and conceal pride from man, He keeps back his soul from the Pit, and his life from perishing by the sword.

Then He is gracious to him, and says,

24 'Deliver him from going down to the Pit; I have found a ransom'; his flesh shall be young like a child's, he shall return to the days of his youth. He shall pray to God, and He will delight in him, he shall see His face with joy, for He restores to man his righteousness."

In the Bible, redemption and healing are together.

The greatest chapter is Isaiah 53, verse 4.

"carried" = substitute. Not "carry with his hands," but He destroyed it.

He bore our sin.

Forgiveness and healing are both truths of the gospel

How do you know you are saved? The Holy Spirit spoke to us through our spirit man. We know that we are saved so much that we would die for it.

Yout, many teachers today oppose the truth of divine healing, causing people not to believe that God wants to heal us, a truth just as solid as forgiveness and redemption.

Matthew 8:17 confirms Isaiah – "And He cast out the spirits with a word, and healed all who were sick, that it might be fulfilled which was spoken by Isaiah the prophet, saying: 'He Himself took our infirmities, And bore our sicknesses.'" (Isaiah 53:4)

Our nature is to sin. God forgives.

Our fallen nature gets sick and has physical pain. God heals.

"With his stripes we are healed" "By his wounds we are healed." – that benefit is in addition to the work of redemption.

"Surely" – one of the strongest words in Hebrew. "I put my oath behind it." The same as the Greek: "Verily, verily."

Sin and sickness, sin and disease have passed from us, to Jesus.

The beginning starts when God reveals your own heart to you.

Isaiah 1 – I am man of unclean lips. Peter saw Jesus and said, "I am a sinner."

The moment we see who we are, we reject it and crucify it.

Revelation: healing and forgiveness are united. Healing is as much a part of salvation as the saving of the soul. Healing is not separate from redemption. A part of redemption is the healing of the body. Jesus on the cross paid for both.

It would be ridiculous to pray, "God, if it is your will, save me."

Yet, many feel that way about healing, which is just as much his will to save. We must get to the level where we believe that God wants to heal us as much as He wants to save us.

We need to preach the healing message like we preach salvation.

The healing ministry will continue throughout the millennium. In the millennium reign of Christ, even the trees will bring healing. The waters that flow from the temple will bring healing. The river will bring healing. Healing will be a part of the kingdom.

It is God's will to heal.

Exodus 15:26 – "I am the God that heals you."

Mark 16:17,18 – "And these signs will follow

those who believe: In My name they will cast out demons; they will speak with new tongues; they will take up serpents; and if they drink anything deadly, it will by no means hurt them; they will lay hands on the sick, and they will recover."

James 5:15 – "And the prayer of faith will save the sick, and the Lord will raise him up. And if he has committed sins, he will be forgiven."

God cannot lie. There is no lie in Him. Numbers 23:19, Malachi 3:6

Satan is a liar and the father of lies. Lies and sin were born in his heart.

The truth is a person – Jesus Christ.

One is total truth and light. One is total lie and darkness.

God Never Changes

Malachi 3:6 – "For I am the LORD, I do not change; therefore you are not consumed, O sons of Jacob."

God is truth. He never changes.

It does not matter what we think, see, believe, etc. There is truth.

Jesus Christ is truth. God is truth. There is no lie in Him. It is impossible for him to lie.

God says, "I am the Lord. I change not." He does not change his word, his covenant. He has magnified his word above his very name.

God's will will be performed.

Jeremiah 51:5 – "For Israel is not forsaken, nor Judah, by his God, the LORD of hosts, though their land was filled with sin against the Holy One of Israel."

Israel was split into two kingdoms. Because of sin, they were driven to Assyria and Babylon. A remnant stayed in the holy land with Jeremiah. God told some not to go to Egypt, but they still went.

Even though their land is filled with sin, and they are gone, God says, "I will not break my promise." This is a God who keeps his covenant when we do not. He will keep his word without you. We are the ones who walk away from him.

Israel said, "We don't want you. We want Baal, or another, or another…"

He will fulfill his word. If his people reject him, he will wait for a new people.

Exodus 15:26 – "I am the God that heals you."

That is eternal. He will be the God who heals you, even if you reject him as healer.

God is truth. His word is truth and eternal whether people hear it or not. He cannot deny himself.

Psalm 89:34 – "My covenant I will not break, nor alter the word that has gone out of My lips."

Psalm 34:19 – "the Lord delivers him out of them all."

He heals all disease and delivers from all afflictions.

We must do our part and believe and trust him.

Jeremiah 1:12 – "Then the LORD said to me,

'You have seen well, for I am ready to perform My word.'"

He stands behind his word with all the power in heaven.

Mark 7:24 – "From there He arose and went to the region of Tyre and Sidon. And He entered a house and wanted no one to know it, but He could not be hidden."

Matthew 15 and,

Mark 7:24 – Jesus wanted no one to know he was in the house. But there was a woman who was determined to get to Jesus. We need to be as determined as that woman in order to receive the anointing. She broke through the door, violated his privacy, and pressed him. He ignored her. When Jesus did not answer her, she went to the disciples and bothered them. The disciples came to him and said 'send her away.' He tells her, 'I am not sent to you. I am sent to the house of Israel.' She begs of him, and lays on the ground. He looks at her and says, 'The bread is only for the children, and not the dogs (Dogs refers to Gentiles)." She admits that she is a dog and that Jews are the masters. He said, "Great is your faith." It was her boldness that moved Jesus.

She understood: I have to press him until he responds; persist, with determination.

He will never say no to those who seek for His healing anointing.

TEN

Truths & Revelations about Healing

The word of God guarantees your healing.

Jesus had 82 healing evangelists on his team. He called the 12 and the 70. With Jesus, there were 83.

Today, there are not many healing evangelists. Why? Because of lack of teaching; lack of knowledge; lack of instruction; and lack of faith.

If He forgives all, he heals all. Believers believe He forgives and saves. We should also believe He heals.

For healing, we must release faith in a different dimension. That person has to do something physically. It's different from forgiveness and salvation.

Key: When it comes to miracles, God waits for

our cooperation.

John 14:9 – Jesus is the express image of God Almighty. He is God's will in action.

He went about healing ALL.

MT 4, 8, 9, 12, Mark 6 – He healed ALL

Jeremiah – God says to Israel, I removed my hand of protection.

Does God allow it? He moves his hands away.

It's our nature to sin and go away from God. He eventually might take his hand away.

Why does sickness come? Because of peoples' ways. Their nature is wicked. They love to do wickedness. That is our nature, our flesh.

We are God's garden, field, farm

God's word will always bring results. We are the ones who do not accomplish anything.

Luke 8:11-12 – "'Now the parable is this: The seed is the word of God. Those by the wayside are the ones who hear; then the devil comes and takes away the word out of their hearts, lest they should believe and be saved.'"

We have to plant our own garden. We have to nourish it.

Some preachers preach using someone else's mantle. But you must have your own.

Elisha ministered under Elijah's mantle. Elisha was one of his prophets. The day came he had to pick up the mantle and use it for God's glory.

Healing ministries especially have the ability

to impart mantles for a season. But those under it have to pick up their own.

We are God's garden. The word is the seed.

1 Corinthians 3:6-9 – "I planted, Apollos watered, but God gave the increase. So then neither he who plants is anything, nor he who waters, but God who gives the increase. Now he who plants and he who waters are one, and each one will receive his own reward according to his own labor. For we are God's fellow workers; you are God's field, you are God's building."

We are God's garden, field, farm.

Mark 4:3-8 – "'Listen! Behold, a sower went out to sow. And it happened, as he sowed, that some seed fell by the wayside; and the birds of the air came and devoured it. Some fell on stony ground, where it did not have much earth; and immediately it sprang up because it had no depth of earth. But when the sun was up it was scorched, and because it had no root it withered away. And some seed fell among thorns; and the thorns grew up and choked it, and it yielded no crop. But other seed fell on good ground and yielded a crop that sprang up, increased and produced: some thirtyfold, some sixty, and some a hundred.'"

We decide what kind of ground we are, for the seed He is throwing on our life.

Be careful what and how you hear

Mark 4:23-24 – "'If anyone has ears to hear,

let him hear.' Then He said to them, 'Take heed what you hear. With the same measure you use, it will be measured to you; and to you who hear, more will be given.'"

Luke – take heed "how" you hear.

Be careful what you hear; be careful how you hear it. Because your life will produce it.

You are responsible for your field and what kind of field you are. God is responsible for the seed.

What do you hear – what do you allow – and how do you allow it in.

The anointing begins with a seed. The farm, the field, the garden has to be plowed and ready. You have to make your garden clean and good ground. You have to nurture the land, plow it, clean it, gets rocks out, with no worldliness and thorns, fertilized.

Acts 20:32 – "So now, brethren, I commend you to God and to the word of His grace, which is able to build you up and give you an inheritance among all those who are sanctified."

The word will build in me and give me an inheritance.

You have to sow it with determination and strength. Hear it and hear it and hear it, until you sow it in the depth of your being.

1 Thessalonians 2:13 – "The word of God which effectually works also in you that believe."

The word is effective. It produces. There is abundance being poured in your soul.

Take heed what you hear. Take heed how you

hear it.

Build up your most holy faith with the word of God. It's building and giving.

Psalm 119:93 – "I will never forget Your precepts, for by them You have given me life."

The word quickens and gives life.

Hebrews 5:13,14 – "For everyone who partakes only of milk is unskilled in the word of righteousness, for he is a babe. But solid food belongs to those who are of full age, that is, those who by reason of use have their senses exercised to discern both good and evil."

We grow from faith to faith.

Seven levels of faith

Romans 12:3 – measure of faith. That measure is inside that seed.

2 Thessalonians 1:3 – this faith develops.

ELEVEN

The Names of God Reveal Healing

A key to God's name is the power of His name in prayer.

Jesus Christ gives us power in His name through prayer.

John 14:13-14: "'And whatever you ask in My name, that I will do, that the Father may be glorified in the Son. If you ask anything in My name, I will do it.'"

John 16:23-24: "'And in that day you will ask Me nothing. Most assuredly, I say to you, whatever you ask the Father in My name He will give you. Until now you have asked nothing in My name. Ask, and you will receive, that your joy may be full.'"

The literal theme of the Bible is the seed and line of the Messiah. Anything connected to the Messiah is mentioned; if something is not connected, it is not mentioned.

The Bible is written about redemption and about Christ being revealed. Within this theme, there are seven dispensations (a system of order or government).

Adamic
Noahic
Abrahamic
Mosaic
Davidic
Messianic
Everlasting

These dispensations include the dispensations of Innocence, Promise, Law, Government, Promise, Grace, and so forth. They connect and are related.

For example, the Era of Promise, Abraham's era, brought the law.

Genesis 12:2 – God promised Abraham, saying "I will bless you and make you a blessing." God revealed the Gospel to him; how? God was telling him, "I will make you a blessing through your seed, Christ." He received the promise of the Messiah.

Why was the law given? To reveal to man his need for a promised Messiah. Sin had been born in his heart. Sin came from Satan's heart. See

Ezekiel 28. The first sin was jealousy. Isaiah 14 explains that Satan tried to invade heaven and was cast out.

Satan corrupted the heart of man, who was given dominion over the earth and was given a kingdom. Sin entered man's heart. His and her nature changed. They became sinful. But man did not know it until the law came. They only knew they were sinful when the law said, "You shall not murder, lie, covet, etc." The law revealed sin. The law is holy. The law is good. The law revealed how sinful they were.

The promise was that a redeemer would come. God revealed the messiah before his need for a messiah, before the law. Jesus ministered in the dispensation of law, which continued until the blood was shed.

Hebrews 3 – we have a better covenant built on better promises.

The Names of God

Elohim – Mighty God, the Creator
Jehovah – the Lord God, God of Covenant, of relationship; first seen in Genesis 2:4 and 2:7. FYI: there was a covenant God made with the earth (verse 4).

The Names of God: Noah and the Animals
Genesis 7,8 – God tells Noah to bring animals into the ark. When God tells him take in the unclean animals two by two, we see the name

Twelve Names of God

Elohim – The Creator, the Mighty One – Genesis 1:1

Jehovah Elohim – Father – Genesis 2:4

El Shaddai – Nourisher, Provider – Genesis 17:1

Adonai – Lord – Genesis 15:1-2

Jehovah Jireh – Provider – Genesis 22:14

Jehovah Rapha – Healer – Exodus 15:26

Jehovah Nissi – Victory – Exodus 17:15

Jehovah Mikkadesh – Holiness – Leviticus 20:7-8

Jehovah Shalom – Peace – Judges 6:24

Jehovah Rohi – Shepherd – Psalm 23:1

Jehovah Tsidkenu – Righteousness – Jeremiah 23:6

Jehovah Shamah – the Lord is there – Ezekiel 48:3

Elohim used. When God tells him to take in the clean animals seven by seven for sacrifice, we see the name Jehovah used.

The name Jehovah is used in connection to relationship and covenant.

The Name of Jesus – when we say the name of Jesus in prayour, we bring that mighty name where we are.

El-Shaddai – Genesis 17 – the revelation of this name changed Abram's name to Abraham.
"I am the Almighty God, walk before Me . . ." The word for Almighty there in Hebrew is "El Shaddai." With that name he promised multiplication. The name El Shaddai is always connected to multiplication and blessings. The name brings transformation.

The name Jehovah was NOT revealed to Abraham. It's one of the most amazing truths found in the Bible.

Exodus 6:3 – "And God spoke to Moses and said to him: 'I am the LORD. I appeared to Abraham, to Isaac, and to Jacob, as God Almighty, but by My name LORD I was not known to them.'"

Adonai – Genesis 18 – He reveals Himself as Lord, your owner.
Genesis 18:17 – "And the LORD said, "Shall I hide from Abraham what I am doing,
When you know him as "My Lord," he will

hide nothing from you. Revelation.

You become a co-partner and co-laborer with him.

This revelation produces intercessors.

Abraham became the great intercessor. He began to intercede for Sodom and Gomorrah.

Elohim – The Almighty, Creator; power, might, and acts

Jehovah – Our Father

El Shaddai – My Nourishment and Supply

Adonai – My Lord who hides nothing from me; revelation. He owns my life and soul. I become His slave and servant.

Jehovah-Jireh – My Provision

Genesis 22:14 – this speaks of Jesus Christ.

It is in Jehovah Jireh we see Christ.

Jesus said, "Abraham saw my day." That's in Genesis 22

Abraham was about to sacrifice Isaac, and the Lord provided a lamb. This is about God's provision for humanity. It's about providing salvation, redemption. It's not about material provision. Abraham SAW God providing Himself a lamb. "God will provide Himself a lamb." The Messiah was revealed.

After that revelation of Christ, He heals my body. He cannot be your Healer until you see Christ. You have to follow the order.

Jehovah Rapha – Exodus 15:26 – the result of Jesus being revealed.

Numbers 21 – whosoever looks shall live. Healing is the result of seeing Jesus.

Jehovah Nissi – My Victory – Exodus 17:15
Seeing Jesus brings healing and victory

Jehovah Mikkadesh – His Holiness, Sanctity – Leviticus 20:7,8
Now we live in holiness

Jehovah Shalom – My Peace – Judges 6:24

Jehovah Rohi – my Shepherd – Psalm 23:1
He leads me in paths of r'ss. Once you meet him as my shepherd, the next revelation is . . .

Jehovah Tsidkenu – my Righteousness – Jeremiah 23:6
His r'ss brings His glory. His presence is now here.

Jehovah Shamah – the Lord is there; the Glory of the Lord is there- Ezekiel 48:3

The name of **Jesus Christ** brings God on the scene, in His fullness. You bring the very nature of God, the glory of God, the supply of God, every one of the revelations of God in these 12 revelations. Power, covenant, and on and on.
When he shows up, his enemies flee. Sickness flees.
He has promised divine health.

TWELVE

Notes

Psalm 105:37 – Not one person was sick, out of 3 million people. This is the greatest health report in human history.

Sickness only exists in Egypt, a type of the world.

Exodus 23:25 – "I will take sickness away from the midst of you." They knew sickness. What brought health to them?

Proverbs 3:7 – Do not be wise in your own eyes; fear the LORD and depart from evil. 8 It will be health to your flesh, and strength to your bones.

Proverbs 4:21,22 – My son, give attention to my words; Incline your ear to my sayings. Do not let them depart from your eyes; keep them in the midst of your heart; for they are life to those who find them, and health to all their flesh.

Jeremiah 30:17 - "'For I will restore health to you And heal you of your wounds,' says the LORD."

Psalm 91

God's presence brings health. He drives away sickness.

Psalm 103 – God's presence and His ways are one. When sin entered in, they got sick. Moses did not know sickness because he knew His ways.

Jesus healed all and refused none

Jesus healed all:
MT 4:23-24, MT 8:16, MT 12:15, MT 15:30-31, MT 21:14, LK 6:17-19, LK 5:15, LK 7:21, LK 9:11

MT 8:16 – He healed all

MT 9:35 – He healed all

MT 12:15 – He healed all

Acts 5:14-16

It is God's will to heal all.

Jesus healed all. He even healed man who betrayed Him. John 5

Jesus wanted those following him to stay healed – he feed the large crowd "that they may not faint on the way." - Matthew 15:32

God is the God of abundance – John 10:10

Our body is the temple of the Spirit. Our body should not have sin or sickness.

Union with the Lord brings forth holiness. We

become partakers of his holiness. This temple should not be sick.

Job 5:26 – You shall come to the grave at a full age,

As a sheaf of grain ripens in its season.

Divine health is promised to us.

Acts 5:16 – Jesus healed all through the apostles.

How to keep your healing

Sickness is the result of sin.

Sin caused the fallen state of mankind and the earth. It hurt mankind, also the animals.

Ezekiel 28 – about Satan, "You were perfect in all your ways, til iniquity was found in you." Sin began in the heart of Lucifer.

Ground must be taken forcefully by faith from the devil, the enemy. He is watching for an occasion to take ground back, which he lost.

We are in a battle. Paul wrote, "I have fought the good fight . . ."

Deuteronomy 1:8

The land is before you. Now go and take it.

Deuteronomy 1:26

The land is before you. Go possess it. Don't be afraid or discouraged. And I WILL GO WITH YOU. The Lord will fight.

Deuteronomy 2:24 – Rise up, and pass over the river.

Begin to possess it by fighting for it.

"I will put the dread and fear of you in the

kingdom of darkness." Your fighting will put fear and dread in the kingdom of darkness.

Job 1:5 - Job applied the blood

Job 1:10 – there is a hedge around of protection around Job, and the devil cannot touch him.

The blood is your protection.

Ecclesiastes 10:8 – He who digs a pit will fall into it,

And whoever breaks through a wall will be bitten by a serpent.

If there is no hedge around you, the serpent will bite you.

How Demons Operate

Matthew 12:43-45

"When an unclean spirit goes out of a man, he goes through dry places, seeking rest, and finds none. Then he says, 'I will return to my house from which I came.' And when he comes, he finds it empty, swept, and put in order. Then he goes and takes with him seven other spirits more wicked than himself, and they enter and dwell there; and the last state of that man is worse than the first. So shall it also be with this wicked generation."

1. They can move, travel. They leave someone's house and go to another one.
2. They seek and search. They listen. They are seeking rest in someone's body.
3. They can speak.

4. They have a will.
5. They can think and make decisions. They are beings with intelligence.
6. They have faith and believe they will go back into the house they were in.
7. They have memory.
8. They examine a person's life.
9. They can plan – "Then he goes . . ."
10. They know how to bring other devils

Jesus Christ offers total liberty from the enemy. John 8:36 – "Therefore if the Son makes you free, you shall be free indeed."

Jesus is the secret place.

John 5:14 – Jesus told man, "Sin no more, lest a worse thing come to you." Sin is an open invitation to the enemy.

If someone's physical ailment is caused by a demon, when that demon is cast out, he will try to come back with other demons. Resist the devil, and he will flee from you.

Deut. 1 – possess with a battle, a fight

1 Peter 5:9 – we resist the enemy in the faith

Jesus did not resist the devil with His experience. He resisted him with the word.

The sword of the Spirit, which is the word of God.

How to Protect Yourself Against Demons

1. Build a hedge
2. Be filled with the Spirit, put on the new man

3. Resist the enemy with the word

4. Live in an atmosphere of faith – example: attend a spirit-filled church

Find food for your faith – it is found where there is an atmosphere of faith

Isaiah 5:12

People deny his power, are gone into captivity. They have no knowledge. Men are famished and multitude is drying up with thirst. They deny God's power. When power of God is denied, people go into captivity.

Jeremiah 10:20,21 –

The pastors have become brutish and have not sought the Lord. Why are churches not growing? Pastors are not praying.

Jeremiah 12:10,11 –

Luke 4:38 – woman was healed, then testified to them after

Luke 17:11-19 – the story of the 10 lepers. Jesus took notice; "were not ten healed, but only one came back." Look at this man who is testifying of his miracle.

Mark 5:19 – "Go home and tell you friends what great things the Lord has done for you."

Revelation 12:11 – they overcame him by the blood and the word of their testimony.

"Every time I testify, demons are driven back."

Keep your eyes on Jesus.

THIRTEEN

Healing Scriptures in Every Book of the Bible

So God created man in his own image, in the image of God created He him; male and female created he them.
(Genesis 1:27)

And God said, 'If you will diligently listen to the voice of the LORD your God, and will do that which is right in His sight, and will give ear to His commandments, and keep all His statutes, I will put none of these diseases upon you, which I have brought upon the Egyptians: for I am the LORD that heals you.'
(Exodus 15:26)

And God said, 'So you shall serve the Lord your God, and He will bless your bread and

your water. And I will take sickness away from the midst of you. No one shall suffer miscarriage or be barren in your land; I will fulfill the number of your days.'
(Exodus 23:25-26)

But if the priest comes in and examines it, and indeed the plague has not spread in the house after the house was plastered, then the priest shall pronounce the house clean, because the plague is healed.
(Leviticus 14:48)

Then the Lord said to Moses, 'Make a fiery serpent, and set it on a pole; and it shall be that everyone who is bitten, when he looks at it, shall live.'
(Numbers 21:8)

And the Lord will take away from you all sickness, and will afflict you with none of the terrible diseases of Egypt which you have known, but will lay them on all those who hate you.
(Deuteronomy 7:15)

Moses was one hundred and twenty years old when he died. His eyes were not dim nor his natural vigor diminished.
(Deuteronomy 34:7)

And now, behold, the Lord has kept me alive, as He said, these forty-five years, ever since the

Lord spoke this word to Moses while Israel wandered in the wilderness; and now, here I am this day, eighty-five years old. As yet I am as strong this day as on the day that Moses sent me; just as my strength was then, so now is my strength for war, both for going out and for coming in.
(Joshua 14:10-11)

Then the Lord said to him, 'Peace be with you; do not fear, you shall not die.' So Gideon built an altar there to the Lord, and called it The-Lord-Is-Peace. To this day it is still in Ophrah of the Abiezrites.
(Judges 6:23-24)

But she said to them, 'Do not call me Naomi; call me Mara, for the Almighty has dealt very bitterly with me.'
(Ruth 1:20)

Then the women said to Naomi, 'Blessed be the Lord, who has not left you this day without a close relative; and may his name be famous in Israel! And may he be to you a restorer of life and a nourisher of your old age; for your daughter-in-law, who loves you, who is better to you than seven sons, has borne him.'
(Ruth 4:14-15)

And he had two wives; the name of the one was Hannah, and the name of the other Peninnah: and Peninnah had children, but Hannah had no children.

And she vowed a vow, and said, O LORD of hosts, if you will indeed look on the affliction of your handmaid, and remember me, and not forget your handmaid, but will give to your handmaid a male child, then I will give him to the LORD all the days of his life, and no razor shall come upon his head.

And they rose up in the morning early, and worshiped before the Lord, and returned, and came to their house to Ramah: and Elkanah knew Hannah his wife; and the Lord remembered her.

Then it came to pass, when the time was come about after Hannah had conceived, that she bore a son, and called his name Samuel, saying, Because I have asked him of the Lord.

(1 Samuel 1:2, 11, 19-20)

We must all die; we are like water spilled on the ground, which cannot be gathered up again. And God does not take away life, but devises means so that he who is banished may not be an utter outcast from Him.

(2 Samuel 14:14)

And it came to pass after these things, that the son of the woman, the mistress of the house, fell sick; and his sickness was so sore, that there was no breath left in him.

And she said to Elijah, 'What have I to do with you, O you man of God? Have you come to me to remind me of my sin, and to slay my son?'

And he stretched himself upon the child three times, and cried to the Lord, and said, 'Lord my God, I pray, let this child's soul come into him again.'

And the Lord heard the voice of Elijah; and the soul of the child came into him again, and he was revived.

(1 Kings 17:17-18, 21-22)

Then went he down, and dipped himself seven times in Jordan, according to the saying of the man of God: and his flesh became like the flesh of a little child, and he was clean.

(2 Kings 5:14)

Then there went certain, and told David how the men were served. And he sent to meet them: for the men were greatly ashamed. And the king said, 'Wait at Jericho until your beards are grown, and then return.'

(1 Chronicles 19:5)

And in the thirty-ninth year of his reign, Asa became diseased in his feet, and his malady was severe; yet in his disease he did not seek the Lord, but the physicians.

So Asa rested with his fathers; he died in the forty-first year of his reign.

(2 Chronicles 16:12-13)

And now for a little while grace has been shown

from the Lord our God, to leave us a remnant to escape, and to give us a peg in His holy place, that our God may enlighten our eyes and give us a measure of revival in our bondage.

For we were slaves. Yet our God did not forsake us in our bondage; but He extended mercy to us in the sight of the kings of Persia, to revive us, to repair the house of our God, to rebuild its ruins, and to give us a wall in Judah and Jerusalem.
(Ezra 9:8-9)

Then he said to them, 'Go your way, eat the fat, drink the sweet, and send portions to those for whom nothing is prepared; for this day is holy to our Lord. Do not sorrow, for the joy of the Lord is your strength.'
(Nehemiah 8:10)

The days on which the Jews had rest from their enemies, as the month which was turned from sorrow to joy for them, and from mourning to a holiday; that they should make them days of feasting and joy, of sending presents to one another and gifts to the poor.
(Esther 9:22)

Then He is gracious to him, and says, 'Deliver him from going down to the Pit; I have found a ransom'; His flesh shall be young like a child's, He shall return to the days of his youth. He shall pray to God, and He will delight in him, He shall see His face with joy, For He restores

to man His righteousness. Then he looks at men and says, 'I have sinned, and perverted what was right, and it did not profit me.' He will redeem his soul from going down to the Pit, and his life shall see the light.
(Job 33:24-28)

He sent His word and healed them,
And delivered them from their destructions.
(Psalm 107:20)

My son, attend to my words; incline your ear to my sayings.
Let them not depart from your eyes; keep them in the midst of your heart.
For they are life to those that find them, and health to all their flesh.
(Proverbs 4:20-22)
Bless the LORD, O my soul, and forget not all his benefits:
Who forgives all your iniquities; who heals all your diseases;
(Psalm 103:2-3)

Pleasant words are as an honeycomb, sweet to the soul, and health to the bones.
(Proverbs 16:24)

A merry heart does good like a medicine: but a broken spirit dries up the bones.
(Proverbs 17:22)

A time to kill, and a time to heal; a time to break down, and a time to build up;
(Ecclesiastes 3:3)

Who is she that looks forth as the morning, fair as the moon, clear as the sun, and terrible as an army with banners?
(Song of Solomon 6:10)

Surely He has borne our griefs, and carried our sorrows: yet we did esteem Him stricken, smitten of God, and afflicted.
But He was wounded for our transgressions, He was bruised for our iniquities: the chastisement of our peace was upon Him; and with His stripes we are healed.
(Isaiah 53:4-5)

'For I will restore health to you, and I will heal you of your wounds,' says the LORD; 'because they called you an Outcast, saying, "This is Zion, whom no man seeks after."'
(Jeremiah 30:17)

Let us search and try our ways, and turn again to the LORD.
Let us lift up our heart with our hands to God in the heavens.
(Lamentations 3:40-41)

Then he said to me: 'This water flows toward the eastern region, goes down into the valley,

and enters the sea. When it reaches the sea, its waters are healed. And it shall be that every living thing that moves, wherever the rivers go, will live. There will be a very great multitude of fish, because these waters go there; for they will be healed, and everything will live wherever the river goes.'
(Ezekiel 47:8-9)

Then Nebuchadnezzar came near to the mouth of the burning fiery furnace, and said, 'Shadrach, Meshach, and Abednego, you servants of the Most High God, come forth, and come here.' Then Shadrach, Meshach, and Abednego, came out of the midst of the fire.
(Daniel 3:26)

I will heal their backsliding, I will love them freely: for My anger is turned away from him.
(Hosea 14:4)

And I will restore to you the years that the locust has eaten, the cankerworm, and the caterpillar, and the palmerworm, My great army which I sent among you.
(Joel 1:25)

'On that day I will raise up the tabernacle of David, which has fallen down, and repair its damages; I will raise up its ruins, and rebuild it as in the days of old; that they may possess the remnant of Edom, and all the Gentiles who

are called by My name,' says the Lord who does this thing. 'Behold, the days are coming,' says the Lord, 'When the plowman shall overtake the reaper, and the treader of grapes him who sows seed; the mountains shall drip with sweet wine, and all the hills shall flow with it. I will bring back the captives of My people Israel; they shall build the waste cities and inhabit them; they shall plant vineyards and drink wine from them; they shall also make gardens and eat fruit from them. I will plant them in their land, and no longer shall they be pulled up from the land I have given them,' says the Lord your God.
(Amos 9:11-15)

But upon mount Zion shall be deliverance, and there shall be holiness; and the house of Jacob shall possess their possessions.
(Obadiah 17)

So the people of Nineveh believed God, and proclaimed a fast, and put on sackcloth, from the greatest of them even to the least of them.

For word came to the king of Nineveh, and he arose from his throne, and he laid his robe from him, and covered him with sackcloth, and sat in ashes.

And he caused it to be proclaimed and published through Nineveh by the decree of the king and his nobles, saying, Let neither man nor beast, herd nor flock, taste any thing: let them not feed, nor drink water:

But let man and beast be covered with sackcloth, and cry mightily to God: let them turn every one from his evil way, and from the violence that is in their hands.

Who can tell if God will turn and repent, and turn away from His fierce anger, that we perish not?

And God saw their works, that they turned from their evil way; and God repented of the evil, that He had said that He would do to them; and He did not do it.

(Jonah 3:5-10)

Therefore I will look to the Lord; I will wait for the God of my salvation; My God will hear me. Do not rejoice over me, my enemy; When I fall, I will arise; When I sit in darkness, the Lord will be a light to me.

(Micah 7:7-8)

Your injury has no healing, your wound is severe. All who hear news of you, will clap their hands over you, for upon whom has not your wickedness passed continually?

(Nahum 3:19)

Sing, O daughter of Zion! Shout, O Israel!
Be glad and rejoice with all your heart,
O daughter of Jerusalem!
The Lord has taken away your judgments,
He has cast out your enemy.
The King of Israel, the Lord, is in your midst;

You shall see disaster no more.
In that day it shall be said to Jerusalem:
"Do not fear;
Zion, let not your hands be weak.
The Lord your God in your midst,
The Mighty One, will save;
He will rejoice over you with gladness,
He will quiet you with His love,
He will rejoice over you with singing."
"I will gather those who sorrow over the appointed assembly,
Who are among you,
To whom its reproach is a burden.
Behold, at that time
I will deal with all who afflict you;
I will save the lame,
And gather those who were driven out;
I will appoint them for praise and fame
In every land where they were put to shame.
(Zephaniah 3:14-19)

Then Haggai, the Lord's messenger, spoke the Lord's message to the people, saying, "I am with you, says the Lord."
(Haggai 1:13)

And the Lord said to me, "Next, take for yourself the implements of a foolish shepherd. For indeed I will raise up a shepherd in the land who will not care for those who are cut off, nor seek the young, nor heal those that are broken, nor feed those that still stand. But he will eat the

flesh of the fat and tear their hooves in pieces.
(Zechariah 11:15-16)

But to you that fear my name shall the Sun of righteousness arise with healing in his wings; and you shall go forth, and grow up as calves of the stall.
(Malachi 4:2)

And it happened that the father of Publius lay sick of a fever and dysentery. Paul went in to him and prayed, and he laid his hands on him and healed him. So when this was done, the rest of those on the island who had diseases also came and were healed.
(Acts 28:8-9)

And do not be conformed to this world, but be transformed by the renewing of your mind, that you may prove what is that good and acceptable and perfect will of God.
(Romans 12:2)

But the manifestation of the Spirit is given to each one for the profit of all: for to one is given the word of wisdom through the Spirit, to another the word of knowledge through the same Spirit, to another faith by the same Spirit, to another gifts of healings by the same Spirit, to another the working of miracles, to another prophecy, to another discerning of spirits, to another different kinds of tongues, to another

the interpretation of tongues. But one and the same Spirit works all these things, distributing to each one individually as He wills.
(1 Corinthians 12:7-11)

Now all things are of God, who has reconciled us to Himself through Jesus Christ, and has given us the ministry of reconciliation, that is, that God was in Christ reconciling the world to Himself, not imputing their trespasses to them, and has committed to us the word of reconciliation. Now then, we are ambassadors for Christ, as though God were pleading through us: we implore you on Christ's behalf, be reconciled to God.
(2 Corinthians 5:18-20)

Christ has redeemed us from the curse of the law, being made a curse for us: for it is written, Cursed is every one that hangs on a tree:
(Galatians 3:13)

That He would grant you, according to the riches of His glory, to be strengthened with might through His Spirit in the inner man, that Christ may dwell in your hearts through faith; that you, being rooted and grounded in love, may be able to comprehend with all the saints what is the width and length and depth and height— to know the love of Christ which passes knowledge; that you may be filled with all the fullness of God.
(Ephesians 3:16-19)

Since he was longing for you all, and was distressed because you had heard that he was sick. For indeed he was sick almost unto death; but God had mercy on him, and not only on him but on me also, lest I should have sorrow upon sorrow, 30 because for the work of Christ he came close to death, not regarding his life, to supply what was lacking in your service toward me.
(Philippians 2:26-27,30)

Giving thanks to the Father who has qualified us to be partakers of the inheritance of the saints in the light. He has delivered us from the power of darkness and conveyed us into the kingdom of the Son of His love.
(Colossians 1:12-13)

And the very God of peace sanctify you wholly; and I pray God your whole spirit and soul and body be preserved blameless to the coming of our Lord Jesus Christ.
(1 Thessalonians 5:23)

That the name of our Lord Jesus Christ may be glorified in you, and you in him, according to the grace of our God and the Lord Jesus Christ.
(2 Thessalonians 1:12)

Who wishes all men to be saved and [increasingly] to perceive and recognize and discern and know precisely and correctly the [divine] Truth.

(I Timothy 2:4, Amplified Bible)

For God has not given us the spirit of fear; but of power, and of love, and of a sound mind.
(1 Timothy 1:7)

For the grace of God that brings salvation has appeared to all men.
(Titus 2:11)

If then you consider me a partner and a comrade in fellowship, welcome and receive him as you would [welcome and receive] me.
And if he has done you any wrong in any way or owes anything [to you], charge that to my account.
(Philemon 17-18, Amplified Bible)

And make straight paths for your feet, so that what is lame may not be dislocated, but rather be healed.
(Hebrews 12:13)

And the prayer of faith shall save the sick, and the Lord shall raise him up.
(James 5:15)

Who Himself bore our sins in His own body on the tree, that we, having died to sins, might live for righteousness—by whose stripes you were healed.
(1 Peter 2:24)

According as His divine power has given to us all things that pertain to life and godliness, through the knowledge of Him that has called us to glory and virtue:
(2 Peter 1:3)

He that commits sin is of the devil; for the devil sinned from the beginning. For this purpose the Son of God was manifested, that he might destroy the works of the devil.
(1 John 3:8)

For many imposters (seducers, deceivers, and false leaders) have gone out into the world, men who will not acknowledge (confess, admit) the coming of Jesus Christ (the Messiah) in bodily form. Such a one is the imposter (the seducer, the deceiver, the false leader, the antagonist of Christ) and the antichrist.
Look to yourselves (take care) that you may not lose (throw away or destroy) all that we and you have labored for, but that you may [persevere until you] win and receive back a perfect reward [in full].
(2 John 7-8, Amplified Bible)

Beloved, I wish above all things that you may prosper and be in health, even as your soul prospers.
(3 John 2)

But these speak evil of whatever they do not

know; and whatever they know naturally, like brute beasts, in these things they corrupt themselves.

These are spots in your love feasts, while they feast with you without fear, serving only themselves. They are clouds without water, carried about[c] by the winds; late autumn trees without fruit, twice dead, pulled up by the roots;

Now to Him who is able to keep you from stumbling, and to present you faultless, before the presence of His glory with exceeding joy,

(Jude 10, 12, 24)

In the middle of its street, and on either side of the river, was the tree of life, which bore twelve fruits, each tree yielding its fruit every month. The leaves of the tree were for the healing of the nations.

(Revelation 22:2)

Abbreviated Subject Index

Seven reasons Jesus healed, 17
Eight reasons why believers get sick, 18
The eagle: symbol of how someone can be healed instantly, 20
Isaiah 53 and explanation, 26-28
Summary of Ephesians 1, 31
Triple cure for man: spirit, soul, body, 32, 33
Explanation of the Passover, 36
How to receive divine health, 39
How to receive healing, 40, 41
Tabernacle's Three Parts Representing the Three Parts of Man, 42
Faith and healing, 54
The cross brings healing, 59
Eight (8) objections to healing, 62
Objections one through eight, 62-69
We are God's garden, 78
Twelve Names of God, 84
Names of God and Healing, 83-86
Jesus healed all, scripture references, 89
How to keep your healing, 90
How demons operate, 91
How to protect yourself against demons, 92
Healing scriptures from every book of the Bible, 94-111

Bibliography

Osborne, T. L. "Healing the Sick" (Tulsa, OK: Harrison House, 1992)

Hinn, Benny. "Divine Healing" Teaching Series (Dallas, TX: Clarion Call Marketing, 2006)

Lockyour, Herbert. *All the Promises of the Bible* (Grand Rapids, MI: Zondervan, 1962)

Harwell, Jim, edited by. *Jesus Christ's Promises* (Nashville: Bridge Books, 2016)

Kenyon, E. W. "Jesus the Healer" (Tulsa, OK: Harrison House, 1989)

Also from Bridge Books:

Heaven: 33 Stories from a Real Place
Jesus Christ's Promises
War in the Heavens
Faith is Easy

Bridge Ministries exists to exalt the Lord Jesus Christ. Learn more at BridgeMinistries.org.

www.ingramcontent.com/pod-product-compliance
Lightning Source LLC
Chambersburg PA
CBHW071259040426
42444CB00009B/1791